MASTERING YOUR MONEY: A COMPLETE GUIDE TO BUDGETING AND SAVING FOR A VICTORIOUS LIFE

Contents

4

8

Introduction:

In the powerful scene of the present world, where monetary solidness assumes a vital part in deciding the personal satisfaction, excelling at planning and saving is a basic expertise. Whether you are simply leaving on your expert process, trying to defeat monetary difficulties, or meaning to fabricate a vigorous starting point for the future, the capacity to deal with your funds really is a critical calculate making progress and getting a prosperous life.

This thorough aide is intended to engage you with the information and devices important to assume command over your monetary fate. As we dig into the complexities of planning and saving, we will investigate down to earth advances, key preparation, and an outlook that cultivates monetary achievement. Toward the finish of this excursion, you won't just have a very much made spending plan yet additionally a guide for developing a propensity for saving that will act as a foundation for your future monetary undertakings.

Understanding the Importance of Financial Mastery The Relationship Between Financial Wellness and Life Satisfaction Financial wellness encompasses more than just financial transactions; it is unpredictably woven into the texture of our regular routines. Concentrates reliably feature the relationship between's monetary strength and generally life fulfillment. Whether the genuine serenity accompanies having a backup stash or the opportunity to seek after your interests without the heaviness of obligation, dominating your funds establishes the groundwork for a satisfying and effective life.

The Effect of Planning and Saving money on Mental Prosperity

Monetary pressure is an unavoidable issue influencing individuals around the world. The capacity to deal with your cash successfully adds to your monetary wellbeing as well as essentially influences your psychological prosperity. A well-organized budget gives you a sense of control and direction, which helps you feel less anxious and have a better relationship with money.

Making a Plan for Your Money: Laying out Objectives

Transient Objectives: Building a Strong Groundwork

The excursion towards monetary achievement starts with defining reachable momentary objectives. Laying out a backup stash is a basic initial step, giving a security net to unanticipated conditions. At the same time, tending to exorbitant interest obligations guarantees that you're not troubled by superfluous monetary strain.

Medium-Term Objectives: Putting resources into Your Future

As you oversee quick monetary worries, center around medium-term objectives like putting something aside for significant buys or putting resources into schooling and profession improvement. These achievements push you forward, adjusting your monetary propensities to your desires.

Long-Term Objectives: Sustaining a Safe Future

Building a monetarily secure future includes anticipating the long haul. Utilize employer-sponsored plans, prioritize contributions to retirement savings, and investigate individual retirement accounts. In the later stages of your life, these long-term investments support your financial well-being.

Surveying Your Monetary Scene: It is essential to have a clear understanding of your income in order to construct an effective budget. Tracking Income Sources Distinguish all types of revenue, including your compensation, side hustles, independent work, and any extra income streams. This exhaustive outline makes way for informed monetary navigation.

Examining Costs: Fixed versus Variable

Sorting costs into fixed and variable makes a sensible financial plan. Understanding these differentiations helps with distributing reserves properly.

Distinguishing Ways of managing money

A basic part of monetary dominance is investigating ways of managing money. Routinely following and investigating your consumptions uncover designs, permitting you to recognize regions where costs can be managed or disposed of. This newly discovered mindfulness is an amazing asset for spending plan refinement.

Building Your Monetary Stronghold: Making a Financial plan

Adjusting Pay and Costs

An even financial plan guarantees that your pay surpasses your costs. Distribute reserves decisively to different classes, like lodging, transportation, food, and investment funds. This distribution gives an unmistakable outline of your monetary needs.

Apportioning Assets for a Just-in-case account

Focus on making and keeping a just-in-case account affordable for you. This asset fills in as a monetary support during unanticipated conditions, keeping you from taking advantage of long haul reserve funds or gathering obligation to cover unforeseen costs.

Handling Obligation: A Critical Spending plan Part

Designate extra supports in your financial plan to speed up obligation reimbursement, especially exorbitant interest obligations. Focusing on obligation decrease opens up monetary assets as well as adds to further developed FICO ratings and in general monetary wellbeing.

Bridling the Force of Mechanization: Saving Easily Setting Up Programmed Moves

Mechanization is a strong partner in the journey for monetary dominance. Plan programmed moves to your investment account, guaranteeing a steady and restrained way to deal with saving. This hands-off methodology dispenses with the compulsion to spend prior to saving.

Utilizing Manager Supported Retirement Records

If accessible, add to your manager's retirement plan, particularly on the off chance that there is a matching project. This presents a novel chance to develop your retirement investment funds with extra commitments from your manager, speeding up your advancement towards long haul monetary objectives.

Cutting back the Monetary Excess: Cutting Pointless Costs Auditing Month to month Uses

Occasionally audit your month to month consumptions to distinguish unnecessary costs. While certain costs are fixed, others might be diminished or wiped out by and large. Investigate your ways of managing money and pursue cognizant choices to scale back extravagances that might hinder your monetary advancement.

Arranging Bills for Investment funds

Draw in with specialist co-ops to arrange charges and investigate open doors for cost decrease. Whether it's arranging a lower link bill or renegotiating a credit for better terms, effectively looking for ways of managing costs adds to huge investment funds over the long run.

Defending Your Future: Assembling and Keeping a Backup stash

Beginning Little and Steadily Expanding

Start your secret stash with a reachable objective, for example, $500, and steadily increment the objective as your monetary strength develops. This progressive methodology guarantees that you reliably add to your just-in-case account without overpowering your financial plan.

Devoted Secret stash Record

Keep up with your backup stash in a different record to keep it from being utilized for non-crises. You are protected from life's unexpected turns by this dedicated account, which ensures that your financial safety net remains intact when necessary.

Differentiating Speculations

Enhancement is a critical methodology to relieve risk in your venture portfolio. Spread your speculations across various resource classes, like stocks, bonds, and land, to guarantee that the exhibition of one doesn't unduly influence you're in general monetary wellbeing.

Adjusting and reviewing investments on a regular basis is not a one-time event. Routinely audit and change your venture portfolio in view of changing economic situations, your monetary objectives, and your gamble resilience. This powerful methodology guarantees that your ventures line up with your developing monetary scene.

A Deep rooted Excursion: Ceaselessly Checking and Changing

Month to month financial plan Surveys

Put away opportunity every month to audit your spending plan. Evaluate your advancement, distinguish regions for development, and change your financial plan appropriately. This continuous obligation to monetary checking improves your capacity to adjust to evolving conditions.

Gratifying Financial Achievements
Recognize and celebrate your

financial milestones. Whether it's arriving at a reserve funds achievement or effectively taking care of an obligation, recognizing your advancement persuades you to finish what has been started and builds up sure monetary propensities.

Remaining Informed About Your Funds

Information is power in the domain of individual accounting. Remain informed.

Step 1: Set Financial Goals

The first step toward creating a secure and prosperous financial future is to establish financial goals. By laying out clear goals, you give yourself a guide that directs your monetary choices and activities. Step 1 can be broken down in detail as follows: Put forth Monetary Objectives:

1.1 Momentary Objectives

1.1.1 Backup stash:

Objective: Save 3-6 months of everyday costs.

Rationale: A backup stash goes about as a monetary wellbeing net, giving a cushion to unforeseen costs, for example, health related crises, vehicle fixes, or unexpected employment shortfall.

Activity Steps: Decide your month to month everyday costs and set a practical objective for your secret stash. Start investment funds by designating a particular sum from every check.

1.1.2 Obligation Reimbursement:

Objective: Take care of exorbitant interest obligations (Mastercards, credits).

Rationale: Paying off past commitments opens up monetary assets as well as further develops FICO ratings, preparing for better monetary open doors.

Activity Steps: Recognize exorbitant interest obligations and make an arrangement for sped up reimbursement. Think about the snowball or torrential slide technique, contingent upon your inclination.

1.2 Goals for the Medium Term

1.2.1 Major Purchases:

Objective: Save for significant buys (vehicle, home initial investment).

Rationale: Building an asset for tremendous costs guarantees that you can make these buys without falling back on exorbitant loans.

Activity Steps: Determine a savings objective and estimate the purchase's cost. Make a committed investment account for this reason and contribute consistently.

1.2.2 Training and Profession Improvement:

Objective: Put resources into training or profession advancement.

Rationale: Persistent acquiring upgrades your abilities and attractiveness, possibly prompting expanded pay and professional success.

Activity Steps: Recognize important courses, certificates, or studios. Apportion subsidizes in your financial plan for continuous schooling and expert turn of events.

1.3 Long-Term Objectives

1.3.1 Saving for Retirement:

Objective: Contribute routinely to retirement accounts.

Rationale: Anticipating retirement is pivotal for keeping up with monetary autonomy in your later years.

Activity Steps: Investigate boss supported retirement plans (e.g., 401(k)) and individual retirement accounts (IRAs). Put forth a month to month commitment objective in view of your retirement course of events and monetary limit.

1.4 Evaluating and Refining Objectives

1.4.1 Customary Assessment:

Objective: Survey the advancement of your monetary objectives consistently.

Rationale: Ordinary assessments assist you with keeping focused, make important changes, and celebrate accomplishments.

Activity Steps: To evaluate your financial objectives, schedule reviews on a monthly, quarterly, or annual basis. Change targets if necessary and recognize achievements.

1.4.2 Versatility:

Objective: Keep being able to change with life.

Rationale: Life is dynamic, and needs might move. Being versatile permits you to adjust your objectives in light of evolving conditions.

Activity Steps: When major life events occur, like getting married, having kids, or changing careers, you should reevaluate your objectives. Change your monetary arrangement in like manner.

1.5 Mental Parts of Objective Setting

1.5.1 Perception:

Objective: Picture the accomplishment of your monetary objectives.

Rationale: Representation upgrades inspiration and supports the conviction that your objectives are feasible.

Activity Steps: Using visualization techniques or a vision board, visualize the positive outcomes of achieving your financial goals.

1.5.2 Savvy Measures:

Objective: Put forth Shrewd objectives (Explicit, Quantifiable, Reachable, Important, Time-Bound).

Rationale: Savvy objectives give lucidity and concentration, gaining it simpler to follow headway and remain committed.

Activity Steps: Check to see that each financial objective meets the SMART criteria. Change objectives in the event that they are excessively unclear or excessively aggressive.

All in all, putting forth monetary objectives is the foundation of compelling monetary administration. By characterizing clear goals, both present moment and long haul, you engage yourself to pursue informed choices and designate assets decisively. Normal assessment and flexibility are key parts, guaranteeing that your monetary objectives line up with your advancing life conditions.

Step 2: Evaluate Your Pay and Costs

Prior to making a spending plan, having a complete comprehension of your monetary landscape is pivotal. Surveying your pay and costs gives the establishment to viable monetary preparation. This step includes examining different kinds of revenue and ordering your uses

. Here is a definite breakdown of Stage 2:

2.1 Track Your Pay

2.1.1 Work Pay:

Activity Steps: Incorporate all wellsprings of business pay, including your compensation, rewards, and some other types of pay. Consider both pre-expense and post-charge figures for exact planning.

2.1.2 Extra Revenue Sources:

Activity Steps: Distinguish and evaluate any extra revenue sources, like independent work, second jobs, rental pay, or profits from ventures. Guarantee a far reaching outline to catch your total monetary picture.

2.1.3 Income: Regular versus irregular

Activity Steps: Identify the difference between an irregular or variable income and a regular, dependable income. Understanding the steadiness of your pay sources helps in making a sensible financial plan.

2.2 Rundown Your Costs

2.2.1 Fixed Costs:

Activity Steps: Specify fixed costs, including rent or home loan, utilities, insurance installments, advance installments, and membership administrations. These are repeating costs that remain generally consistent every month.

2.2.2 Variable Costs:

Activity Steps: Recognize variable costs like food, eating out, diversion, and optional spending. Variable costs vacillate from one month to another and require cautious following.

2.2.3 Out-of-pocket expenses:

Activity Steps: Represent non-month to month expenses, for example, yearly memberships, local charges, or insurance installments paid quarterly or yearly. Partition these sums by 12 to integrate them into your month to month spending plan.

2.3 Break down Ways of managing money

2.3.1 Order Spending:

Activity Steps: Classify your expenses according to whether they are essential or not. This step recognizes regions where you might possibly scale back or improve spending.

2.3.2 Audit Bank Proclamations:

Activity Steps: Examine your bank and financial records to follow each exchange. This nitty gritty investigation discloses examples and features regions where changes can be made.

2.3.3 Distinguish Hazardous Spending:

Activity Steps: Pinpoint any risky ways of managing money, for example, drive buys or pointless memberships. The first step toward developing better financial habits is awareness.

2.4 Use Planning Apparatuses

2.4.1 Planning Applications:

Activity Steps: Look into budgeting apps and tools that make tracking easier. These devices can give continuous bits of knowledge into your spending examples and assist you with keeping steady over your monetary objectives.

2.4.2 Accounting sheets:

Activity Steps: Create a budget spreadsheet to keep track of expenses and income manually.

This technique offers a nitty gritty, adjustable methodology, permitting you to fit your spending plan to explicit necessities.

2.5 Laying out a Benchmark

2.5.1 Absolute Month to month Pay:

Activity Steps: Sum up your absolute month to month pay by joining all pay sources. This figure fills in as the gauge for planning.

2.5.2 Total Costs Per Month:

Activity Steps: Work out your absolute month to month expenses by including all fixed and variable expenses. Guarantee that your costs don't surpass your pay to keep a fair financial plan.

2.6 Distinguishing Excesses and Shortfalls

2.6.1 Overflows:

Activity Steps: You have a surplus if your income is higher than your expenses. Make strategic use of these additional funds by investing, increasing savings, or paying down debt.

2.6.2 Shortfalls:

Activity Steps: On the off chance that your costs outperform your pay, you have a shortage. Distinguish regions for cost-slicing or consider ways of expanding your pay to bring your spending plan once again into balance.

2.7 Routinely Audit and Change

2.7.1 Month to month Registrations:

Activity Steps: Focus on customary month to month registrations to survey your pay and costs. Change your spending plan depending on the situation in light of changes in pay, costs, or monetary objectives.

2.7.2 Occasional Evaluations:

Activity Steps: Lead occasional evaluations, particularly during significant life altering events like a new position, movement, or huge costs. Adjust your spending plan to line up with your developing monetary conditions.

All in all, surveying your pay and costs is a crucial stage in the planning system. It lays the preparation for informed monetary choices and makes way for making a spending plan that mirrors your monetary reality. Ordinary surveys and changes guarantee that your spending plan stays a dynamic and viable instrument for accomplishing your monetary objectives.

Step 3: Make a Spending plan

Since you have a thorough comprehension of your pay and costs, now is the ideal time to make an interpretation of that information into a down to earth and significant arrangement —

your spending plan. Making a spending plan is a pivotal step towards monetary security and achievement.

Here is a point by point guide on the most proficient method to make a powerful spending plan:

3.1 Adjusting Pay and Costs

3.1.1 Designate Assets to Classes:
Activity Steps: Partition your pay into classes like lodging, transportation, food, reserve funds, and optional spending. Allot explicit sums to every classification in view of your requirements and monetary needs.

3.1.2 Secret stash Allotment:
Activity Steps: Focus on dispensing assets to your secret stash affordable. Consistent contributions to your financial safety net are guaranteed by this.

3.2 Obligation Reimbursement

3.2.1 Obligation Reimbursement Plan:

Activity Steps: To accelerate the repayment of your debt, allocate additional funds to your budget. Depending on your preference and financial objectives, you might want to use either the snowball or avalanche approach.

3.2.2 Least Installments:

Activity Steps: Make sure that your budget includes the minimum payments for all of your debts. This forestalls late expenses and supports your general obligation decrease technique.

3.3 Savings and investments

3.3.1 Contributions to Retirement:

Activity Steps: Distribute a piece of your pay to retirement commitments. Exploit business supported designs and consider extra commitments to individual retirement accounts (IRAs).

3.3.2 Different Investment funds Objectives:

Activity Steps: In the event that you have explicit reserve funds objectives (e.g., significant buys, training), dispense reserves in like manner. Make separate investment accounts for every objective for better association.

3.4 Variable versus Fixed Costs

3.4.1 Fixed Costs:

Activity Steps: Dispense assets for fixed costs like lease, utilities, and protection. These are important expenses that are fairly constant each month.

3.4.2 Variable Costs:

Activity Steps: Distribute assets for variable costs like food, diversion, and feasting out. Be aware of your ways of managing money and put forth practical lines for these classes.

3.5 Checking and Changing

3.5.1 Month to month Surveys:

Activity Steps: Consistently audit your spending plan toward the finish of every month. Contrast genuine enjoying with your planned sums, and distinguish any inconsistencies.

3.5.2 Changes:

Activity Steps: Make acclimations to your financial plan on a case by case basis. In the event that you reliably overspend in a specific class, consider redistributing assets or tracking down ways of diminishing costs.

3.6 Backup stash Contemplations

3.6.1 Need:

Activity Steps: Make contributions to your emergency fund a priority. Treat it as a non-debatable cost to construct a hearty monetary security net.

3.6.2 Occasional Reconsideration:

Activity Steps: Occasionally reevaluate your secret stash objectives. As your monetary circumstance improves, consider expanding the objective sum for added security.

3.7 Planning Apparatuses and Strategies

3.7.1 Advanced Apparatuses:

Activity Steps: Investigate computerized planning devices and applications that can robotize following and give bits of knowledge into your spending designs.

3.7.2 Envelope Framework:

Activity Steps: Think about involving the envelope framework for optional spending classes. Designate actual money to every envelope, and whenever it's gone, try not to spend more in that class.

3.8 Planning for the Long Term

3.8.1 Yearly Planning:

Activity Steps: Think about yearly making arrangements for huge, non-month to month expenses. Planning for these costs consistently guarantees you're monetarily arranged when they emerge.

3.8.2 Objective Reexamination:

Activity Steps: Intermittently rethink your monetary objectives. Make adjustments to your budget in response to shifting priorities, such as saving for a house, school, or other significant life events.

3.9 Look for Proficient Direction

3.9.1 Monetary Guide Discussion:

Activity Steps: If necessary, look for the exhortation of a monetary counsel. They can give customized direction, particularly for complex monetary circumstances or long haul arranging.

3.9.2 Resources for Education:

Activity Steps: Consistently teach yourself on planning best practices and monetary administration. Books, articles, and online assets can ·improve your insight and enable you to settle on informed choices.

In rundown, making a spending plan is a proactive and enabling step towards monetary achievement. Via cautiously dispensing your pay, focusing on obligation reimbursement and reserve funds, and routinely checking and changing your spending plan, you'll be better prepared to accomplish your monetary objectives and fabricate a safe future. Keep in mind that adaptability is essential, and your budget should adapt to your shifting needs and goals.

Step 4: Save Consequently

Programmed investment funds are a strong methodology that guarantees reliable and restrained commitments to your monetary objectives without the requirement for manual intercessions. By setting up programmed moves, you make a propensity for saving that becomes imbued in your monetary everyday practice. Here is a definite aide on the most proficient method to execute programmed investment funds successfully:

4.1 Set Up Programmed Moves

4.1.1 Backup stash Commitments:

Activity Steps: Plan programmed moves from your financial records to your devoted secret stash account. Pick a recurrence (e.g., fortnightly or month to month) that lines up with your compensation plan.

4.1.2 Contributions to Retirement:

Activity Steps: Boost the advantages of manager supported retirement plans by setting up programmed commitments. Exploit highlights like auto-heightening to expand your commitments over the long haul progressively.

4.2 Influence Business Supported Retirement Records

4.2.1 401(k) Commitments:

Activity Steps: On the off chance that your boss offers a 401(k) plan, sign up for the program and set up programmed commitments. Mean to contribute to the point of exploiting any business matching commitments.

4.2.2 Distribution of Direct Deposits:

Activity Steps: On the off chance that conceivable, sort out for a part of your compensation to be straightforwardly stored into your investment account. This guarantees that savings come first, followed by discretionary spending.

4.3 Lay out Investment funds Objectives

4.3.1 Obviously Characterized Goals:

Activity Steps: Obviously characterize your investment funds objectives, whether it's structure a backup stash, putting something aside for a get-away, or adding to a particular speculation. Each goal should be given specific amounts and deadlines.

4.3.2 Programmed Moves for Every Objective:

Activity Steps: Make separate records for various reserve funds objectives and set up programmed moves to each record. This helps keep things organized and makes it clear what each savings pool is for.

4.4 Screen and Change Programmed Moves

4.4.1 Consistently Audit Commitments:

Activity Steps: Occasionally survey the programmed moves to guarantee they line up with your ongoing monetary circumstance and objectives. Change commitment sums as your pay or needs change.

4.4.2 Increment Commitments Over the long haul:

Activity Steps: Slowly increment the programmed commitments to your investment funds. This can be particularly viable after compensation increments or bonuses, assisting you with speeding up progress towards your monetary objectives.

4.5 Backup stash: Putting automatic savings first

4.5.1 Making regular contributions: Activity Steps: Treat your backup stash as really important for programmed reserve funds. Steady commitments, regardless of whether unobtrusive at first, develop after some time and upgrade your monetary security.

4.5.2 Intermittent Reexamination: Activity Steps: Occasionally reevaluate your secret stash objectives. Assuming your monetary circumstance improves or significant life altering events happen, change the programmed commitments to match your refreshed requirements.

4.6 Direct Charge for Obligation Reimbursement

4.6.1 Set Up Programmed Installments:

Activity Steps: In the event that reimbursing obligations is a monetary objective, set up programmed installments for least sums or extra commitments. This guarantees you remain focused with your obligation reimbursement plan.

4.6.2 Paying off debt promptly:

Activity Steps: Opportune installments add to obligation decrease and can get a good deal on interest. Robotize obligation installments to keep away from late expenses and keep a positive record as a consumer.

4.7 Digital Automation Tools

4.7.1 Budgeting Software:

Activity Steps: Use planning applications that offer robotization highlights. These applications can smooth out the most common way of setting up and overseeing programmed moves, giving continuous bits of knowledge into your reserve funds progress.

4.7.2 Alarms and Warnings:

Activity Steps: Enact alarms and warnings from your bank or monetary establishment. Keep track of successful transfers, low balances, and other account irregularities.

4.8 Responsibility and Discipline

4.8.1 Treat Programmed Moves as Non-Debatable:

Activity Steps: Develop the mentality that programmed moves are non-debatable responsibilities to your monetary objectives. Think of them as fixed costs that focus on your future.

4.8.2 Consistently Screen Records:

Activity Steps: Make sure that your planned automatic transfers are taking place by checking your savings and investment accounts on a regular basis. This propensity builds up monetary discipline and mindfulness.

4.9 Change on a case by case basis

4.9.1 Life altering Events:

Activity Steps: Be ready to change programmed moves in light of huge life altering events, for example, work advances, changes in pay, or new monetary objectives.

4.9.2 Intermittent Survey:

Activity Steps: Occasionally audit your generally speaking monetary arrangement, including programmed reserve funds.

Guarantee that your programmed moves line up with your advancing monetary needs.

All in all, saving consequently is a strong and productive method for building monetary security and work towards your monetary objectives. By setting up programmed moves, utilizing business supported retirement designs, and remaining trained in your methodology, you make a manageable and powerful reserve funds system. Routinely screen and change your programmed commitments to keep focused and adjust to evolving conditions. This proactive methodology guarantees that saving turns into a consistent piece of your monetary daily practice, making ready for a safer and prosperous future.

Step 5: Cut Superfluous Costs

Recognizing and cutting pointless costs is an essential move toward improving your spending plan and opening up assets for your monetary objectives. By investigating your ways of managing money and pursuing purposeful decisions, you can divert assets towards reserve funds, obligation reimbursement, or different needs.

Here is an extensive aide on the best way to cut superfluous costs successfully:

5.1 Survey Month to month Costs

5.1.1 Nitty gritty Cost Examination:

Activity Steps: Survey your bank explanations, financial records, and receipts for the beyond couple of months. Sort your expenses into categories to see patterns and learn where your money is going.

5.1.2 What is essential and what is not?

Activity Steps: Separate between unimportant and fundamental costs. Trivial items might incorporate eating out, membership administrations, motivation buys, or superfluous memberships.

5.2 Distinguish Unimportant Costs

5.2.1 Optional Spending:

Activity Steps: Pinpoint areas of optional spending where you have control. This could include things like entertainment, dining out, shopping for things that aren't necessary, or subscriptions that don't give you enough value.

5.2.2 Unused Memberships:

Activity Steps: Recognize and drop any memberships you're not effectively utilizing or profiting from. This could incorporate web-based features, magazine memberships, or participations.

5.3 Arrange Bills for Investment funds

5.3.1 Link and Web:

Activity Steps: Contact your link and internet services to arrange lower rates or investigate elective, more practical plans. Think about cutting link by and large for real time features.

5.3.2 Insurance Installments:

Activity Steps: Search for protection suppliers and contrast statements with guarantee you're getting the best rates. Ask about loyalty or good driver discounts and bundle policies for potential savings.

5.4 Trim Variable Costs

5.4.1 Shopping for food:

Activity Steps: Plan feasts ahead of time, make a shopping rundown, and stick to it. Search for deals, use coupons, and consider nonexclusive brands to eliminate basic food item expenses.

5.4.2 Eat Out:

Activity Steps: Diminish the recurrence of feasting out. Cook at home more regularly, get ready snacks for work, and investigate practical feast arranging techniques.

5.5 Cut Drive Buys

5.5.1 Lay out a Holding up Period:

Activity Steps: Set up a waiting period for purchases that aren't necessary. Give yourself some time to think about whether an item is really necessary or just bought on a whim.

5.5.2 Track Hasty purchases:

Activity Steps: Track drive buys for a month. Examine the list to discover recurring events and triggers. Make use of this knowledge to steer clear of similar unanticipated costs in the future.

5.6 Make a Financial plan for Diversion

5.6.1 Diversion Designations:

Activity Steps: Distribute a particular spending plan for diversion costs. This can incorporate exercises like films, shows, or excursions. Adhere to the financial plan to abstain from overspending.

5.6.2 Investigate Free Other options:

Activity Steps: Search free of charge or minimal expense options for diversion, like local area occasions, outside exercises, or using nearby assets like libraries and parks.

5.7 Arrange Mastercard Loan fees

5.7.1 Contact Mastercard Organizations:

Activity Steps: Try to negotiate lower interest rates with the companies that issue your credit cards. Feature your installment history and ask about any limited time rates or equilibrium move choices.

5.7.2 Investigate Equilibrium Move Choices:

Activity Steps: Assuming you have exorbitant premium Mastercard obligation, investigate balance move choices to cards with lower financing costs. Be aware of move charges and initial period terms.

5.8 Assess Transportation Expenses

5.8.1 Public Transportation:

Activity Steps: In the event that practical, think about utilizing public transportation or carpooling to lessen fuel and support costs related with private vehicle use.

5.8.2 Vehicle Protection:

Activity Steps: Audit your vehicle protection inclusion and investigate amazing open doors for limits. A decent driving record, security highlights, and packaging strategies can bring down charges.

5.9 Look for Limits and Devotion Projects

5.9.1 Devotion Projects:

Activity Steps: Make use of loyalty programs that are offered by retailers or providers of services. Amass focuses or compensates that can be reclaimed for limits or gifts.

5.9.2 Senior, Understudy, or Military Limits:

Activity Steps: Check for limits in light of your status

5.10 Screen and Change Consistently

5.10.1 Month to month Spending plan Surveys:

Activity Steps: Consolidate month to month spending plan audits to keep tabs on your development in cutting pointless costs. Celebrate victories and recognize regions for additional improvement.

5.10.2 Way of life Changes:

Activity Steps: Be available to making way of life changes that line up with your monetary objectives. As you cut superfluous costs, consider what these changes emphatically mean for your by and large monetary prosperity.

5.11 Take into Account DIY Methods

5.11.1 Perform DIY Repairs:

Activity Steps: Acquire fundamental Do-It-Yourself abilities for family fixes and upkeep. This can cut down on the need for professional help and save money on repairs.

5.11.2 Natively constructed Items:

Activity Steps: Think about making specific items at home, like cleaning supplies or individual consideration things. This can be a practical and eco-accommodating other option.

5.12 Keep track of savings and celebrate them

5.12.1 Savings Tracker:

Activity Steps: Create a savings tracker to keep track of the money saved by reducing expenses that aren't necessary. Picturing progress can act as inspiration to keep up with thrifty propensities.

5.12.2 Observe Achievements:

Activity Steps: Celebrate monetary achievements accomplished through cost cutting endeavors. Recognizing accomplishments reinforces good financial habits, whether it's paying off debt or reaching a savings goal.

In conclusion, a proactive strategy for optimizing your budget and redirecting funds toward your financial objectives is to eliminate expenses that are not necessary. Via cautiously examining your ways of managing money, arranging bills, and settling on deliberate decisions, you can make a more productive and intentional monetary arrangement. Routinely audit and change your costs to remain lined up with your changing needs and desires. The excursion to monetary achievement includes acquiring more as well as being aware of how you spend and save.

Step 6: Manufacture and Keep a Stormy day account

Manufacturing and keeping a reinforcement stash is a focal piece of financial consistent quality. A pad against unexpected expenses and difficulties is given by a secret stash, which fills in as a monetary wellbeing net. A thorough aide on the most proficient method to begin and keep a backup stash is given beneath:

6.1 Defining Objectives for a Secret stash

6.1.1 Deciding the Ideal Asset Size:
Action Steps: Assess your month to month ordinary expenses and set forth a goal for your reinforcement stash. For a strong security net, go for the gold a half year of everyday costs.

6.1.2 Consistent Approach:
Movement Steps: Start with a smaller, more manageable amount

(such as one month's expenses) and gradually work your way up to a more ambitious goal if the ideal goal seems overwhelming.

6.2 Picking the Right Record

6.2.1 Separate Ledger:

Action Steps: Open an alternate financial balance dedicated only to your reinforcement stash. This segment hinders accidental spending and ensures holds are actually accessible when required.

6.2.2 Records for Exorbitant Interest Investment funds:

Action Steps: Consider putting your emergency fund in a high-interest savings account. When compared to a standard savings account, interest rates can still provide some additional growth, even if they aren't particularly high.

6.3 Customized Responsibilities

6.3.1 Set Up Customized Moves:

Movement Steps: Plan customized moves from your fundamental monetary records to your blustery day account. This ensures consistent responsibilities and gets rid of the prerequisite for manual trades.

6.3.2 Line up with Pay Schedule:

Movement Steps: Set up moves to agree with your pay plan. This makes adding to your hidden bonanza a steady piece of your financial everyday practice.

6.4 Zeroing in on Responsibilities

6.4.1 Treat as a Non-Begging to be proven wrong Expense:

Movement Steps: Commitments to your just-in-case account ought to be viewed as non-debatable. Treat it with comparable level of importance as paying rent or other fixed costs.

6.4.2 Rewards and Rewards:

Movement Steps: Use rewards, charge limits, or work awards to help your stormy day account. Direct a piece of amazing compensation toward accelerating your headway.

6.5 Looking over and Evolving

6.5.1 Typical Reviews:

Movement Steps: Incidentally overview your blustery day account progress. Change your commitment sum in view of any progressions in everyday costs or pay.

6.5.2 Notice Accomplishments:

Movement Steps: Celebrate milestones reached in your backup stash project. Perceive your achievements, whether they are finishing one month's costs or arriving at half of your objective.

6.6 Use Rewards Definitively

6.6.1 Award Pay:

Action Steps: Distribute a rate directly to your backup stash if you get rewards or commissions on a regular basis. This paces up improvement without influencing your ordinary monetary arrangement.

6.6.2 Monetary Gifts:

Action Steps: Redirect a piece of monetary presents, for instance, birthday or event presents, to your hidden gold mine. This may significantly increase the number of additional commitments.

6.7 Only for Emergencies

6.7.1 Describe Emergency Measures:

Action Steps: Clearly describe what is an emergency. Save the resource exclusively for true surprising circumstances, for instance, clinical expenses, vehicle fixes, or business incident.

6.7.2 Go against Temptation:

Movement Steps: Make an effort not to dive into the in the event represent non-emergencies. The asset's uprightness is improved when its motivation is plainly perceived.

6.8 Redoing After Withdrawals

6.8.1 Fast Restoration Plan:

Action Steps: Think up a technique for rapidly recharging the backup stash if you really want to utilize it. Proceed with modified responsibilities and dispense rewards towards adjusting the resource.

6.8.2 Benefits of Withdrawing:

Movement Steps: Assess the circumstances that incited the prerequisite for withdrawal. Use this data to refine you're in the event account goal or change responsibilities for further developed preparation.

6.9 Theory Considerations

6.9.1 Consistent Change to Adventures:

Movement Steps: At the point when your reinforcement stash shows up at a pleasing level, consider consistently advancing excess resources for the most part safe hypotheses for likely turn of events.

6.9.2 Liquidity versus Returns:

Action Steps: Track down a harmony between the longing for returns and the requirement for liquidity. Ensure that a piece of your hidden bonanza remains really open while examining open entryways for inconspicuous turn of events.

6.10 Incidental Reexamination

6.10.1 Lifestyle Changes:

Movement Steps: Irregularly reevaluate your hidden bonanza goals, especially during basic life changing occasions like marriage, the presentation of a youth.

Step 7: Contribute Keenly

Contributing keenly is an essential piece of money related accomplishment, helping your money with creating for a really long time and making monetary prosperity for what's to come. Sorting out various endeavor decisions, supervising risk, and changing your hypotheses to your financial goals are key pieces of splendid cash the board. A comprehensive guide to the most effective approach to clever contribution is provided here:

7.1 Recognize Your Monetary Targets

7.1.1 Momentary Goals:

Action Steps: Be aware of short-term financial goals, such as saving money for a vacation or a down payment on a house. For transient targets, select fluid, okay speculation choices.

7.1.2 Goals for the Long Term:

Action Steps: For goals with a medium time horizon, like buying a home or sponsoring tutoring, consider a mix of stocks and bonds to change improvement and peril.

7.1.3 Long stretch Goals:

Action Steps: Long stretch goals like retirement require a more intense procedure. Divide a significant amount among differentiated stocks in order to profit from their potential for growth.

7.2 Assess Your Bet Obstruction

7.2.1 Bet Flexibility Evaluation:

Action Steps: Consider how agreeable you are with market variances to decide your gamble resilience. Get hypotheses that line with your bet strength to promise you can remain contributed as far as might be feasible.

7.2.2 Age and Plan for Effective money management:

Action Steps: Hazard might be endured by more youthful financial backers with a more drawn out time skyline. Consider making changes in accordance with your portfolio to save capital as you draw nearer to retirement.

7.3 Make Your Portfolio More Assorted

7.3.1 Resource Assignment:

Action Steps: Expand your wagers on a variety of resource classes, including stocks, bonds, and land. This decreases opportunity and overhauls the potential for stable returns.

7.3.2 Topographical Extension:

Action Steps: Consider interests in different geographic districts to restrict bets related with monetary downturns in unambiguous countries.

7.4 Sort out Different Hypothesis Vehicles

7.4.1 Stocks:

Action Steps: Stocks address ownership in an association. Contemplate them for development over the long haul. Investigate individual stocks or invest in exchanged reserves (ETFs) and expanded shared assets.

7.4.2 Bonds:

Action Steps: Protections of obligation are bonds. They give ordinary interest portions and return the head at advancement. Bonds are generally viewed as lower risk than stocks.

7.4.3 Speculations:

Action Steps: Shared reserves pool funds from various financial backers to invest in a distinct portfolio of stocks, bonds, or other securities. Choose reserves that meet your speculation goals.

7.4.4 ETFs:

Action Steps: Exchange-traded funds (ETFs), like mutual funds, are traded on stock exchanges. They give assortment and are often more prudent.

7.4.5 Property:

Action Steps: Land can be a significant hypothesis through property ownership or a money related adventure through Land

Theory Trusts (REITs). Take a look at your goals and risk tolerance.

7.5 Stay Taught and Educated

7.5.1 Perpetual Learning:

Action Steps: Stay aware of information about ventures, financial pointers, and market patterns. Perpetual learning overhauls your ability to seek after informed hypothesis decisions.

7.5.2 Master Insight:

Action Steps: If essential, search for counsel from money related experts. They can provide tweaked guidance considering your money related situation, targets, and risk strength.

7.6 Set Viable Suppositions

7.6.1 Long stretch Perspective:

Action Steps: Grasp that contributing is a somewhat long attempt. Do whatever it takes not to make decisions considering passing business sector changes.

7.6.2 Execution Previously:

Action Steps: Think about genuine execution while setting presumptions. Nonetheless, you ought to practice alert while depending on past execution to anticipate future results.

7.7 Protection and a Backup stash

7.7.1 Give Need to a Rainy day account:

Action Steps: Before you make huge speculations, verify that your rainy day account is completely supplied. This forestalls the need to sell interests in a crisis.

7.7.2 Enough Insurance:

Action Steps: Include protection for your health, life, and property, which is adequate. This defends your monetary steadiness in case of unanticipated conditions.

7.8 Watch out for and rebalance

7.8.1 Lead intermittent portfolio audits:

Action Steps: Once in a while review your endeavor portfolio to promise it lines up with your goals. If essential, rebalance your portfolio by changing the resource assignment in light of changes on the lookout and moving objectives.

7.8.2 Evaluation Examinations:

Action Steps: Know about obligation ideas while managing your endeavors. Charge useful frameworks can help with restricting the impact on your general returns.

7.9 Averaging by Cost in Dollars

7.9.1 Reliable Commitments:

Action Steps: Execute limiting gamble by dependably adding to your hypotheses over an extended time. This method reduces the impact of market flimsiness on your overall hypothesis.

7.9.2 Adventure Market Plunges:

Action Steps: View market droops as any entryways to buy assets at lower costs. Keep a long perspective and go without making imprudent decisions during market differences.

7.10 Conducting Surveys and Changing

7.10.1 Significant Life Events:

Action Steps: Reevaluate your project methodology from time to time, especially when significant life events occur. Change your portfolio to accommodate your targets, risk resilience, and current monetary circumstance.

7.10.2 Stay Flexible:

Action Steps: Be adaptable to shifts in the financial and business sectors. Stay aware of the news and alter your venture technique in light of changing economic situations.

7.11 Search for Capable Heading

7.11.1 Talk with Money related Insight:

Action Steps: Consult monetary consultants if you're in doubt or managing complex financial circumstances. With their mastery, you can get helpful guidance that is custom fitted to your specific conditions.

7.11.2 Consistent Venture Audit:

Action Steps: Regularly review your theory strategy with a money related expert. This ensures that your technique is still in accordance with your monetary targets and economic situations.

Overall, shrewd contribution is a dynamic and essential cycle that involves careful preparation, constant learning, and adaptability. By changing your theories to your money related targets, keeping a widened portfolio, and staying informed, you can seek after making long stretch monetary energy. Evaluate and change your venture methodology consistently because of changes in your day to day existence, economic situations, and monetary objectives. Keep in mind that contributing is a long-term commitment and that achieving success frequently requires persistent and well-informed guidance.

Step 8: Keeping an eye on your finances and making adjustments

On a regular basis is essential to your long-term success. Life is dynamic, and your monetary circumstance, objectives, and outside variables can change. Consistently checking on and adjusting your procedures guarantees that you remain focused and settle on informed choices. Here is a far reaching guide on the most proficient method to consistently screen and change your monetary arrangement:

8.1 Lay out an Ordinary Survey Timetable

8.1.1 Month to month Registrations: Activity Steps: Put away opportunity every month to survey your spending plan, costs, and progress towards monetary objectives. This successive registration takes into account speedy changes and keeps you mindful of your monetary status.

8.1.2 Quarterly Evaluations:

Activity Steps: Direct more top to bottom evaluations on a quarterly premise. Survey venture portfolios, reserve funds commitments, and any progressions in pay or costs. Reevaluate and reorganize your financial strategy during this time.

8.2 Track Changes in Pay

8.2.1 Yearly Pay Survey:

Activity Steps: Every year survey your pay, representing raises, rewards, or any progressions in work. Change your spending plan and reserve funds commitments as needs be to use expanded pay for monetary objectives.

8.2.2 Other sources of income or side income:

Activity Steps: Assuming you have side pay or extra income streams, routinely survey their effect on your generally speaking monetary picture. Consider enhancing these pay hotspots for greatest advantage.

8.3 Audit and Change Spending plan

8.3.1 Monetary Audits:

Activity Steps: Consistently survey your spending plan to guarantee it mirrors your ongoing monetary needs. Based on changing requirements and objectives, modify spending categories, reallocate funds, and refine your budget.

8.3.2 Just-in-case account Reconsideration:

Activity Steps: Occasionally reevaluate your secret stash objectives. Increase the target amount if your financial situation has improved for added security.

8.4 Survey Obligation Decrease Progress

8.4.1 Obligation Reimbursement Plan Survey:

Activity Steps: Survey your obligation reimbursement plan routinely. Celebrate achievements, reconsider financing costs, and investigate chances to speed up your obligation decrease endeavors.

8.4.2 Union Choices:

Activity Steps: Investigate obligation combination choices assuming it lines up with your monetary objectives. Evaluate the expected advantages, for example, lower financing costs or improved on reimbursement terms.

8.5 Review Savings Objectives

8.5.1 Goal Progress Monitoring:

Activity Steps: Keep tabs on your savings goals' progress. Change courses of events, commitments, or the objective sums in light of your advancing monetary limit and needs.

8.5.2 Look into New Ways to Save Money:

Activity Steps: Distinguish new investment funds open doors or objectives that line up with your desires. Be available to changing your monetary arrangement to oblige these changes.

8.6 Portfolio Evaluations for Investments

8.6.1 Portfolio Performance:

Activity Steps: Routinely survey the exhibition of your venture portfolio. Consider rebalancing if important to keep up with the ideal resource portion.

8.6.2 Economic situations:

Activity Steps: Remain informed about economic situations. Change your venture system in view of monetary patterns, worldwide occasions, and changes in your gamble resistance.

8.7 Way of life Changes and Significant Occasions

8.7.1 Marriage, Births, or Separation:

Activity Steps: Critical life altering situations like marriage, the introduction of a youngster, or separation can influence your monetary arrangement. Rethink objectives, financial plan, and speculation procedures to adjust to these changes.

8.7.2 Work Advances:

Activity Steps: A thorough financial evaluation is required whenever a job is changed, whether through promotions, career shifts, or unemployment. Change your spending plan and reserve funds objectives to line up with your new pay or conditions.

8.8 Protection Inclusion Audit

8.8.1 Life altering Events and Inclusion:

Activity Steps: Consistently audit your protection inclusion, particularly after significant life altering events. Guarantee that arrangements satisfactorily safeguard you and your friends and family.

8.8.2 Shop for Better Rates:

Activity Steps: Intermittently look for better protection rates. There may be opportunities for cost savings in the insurance market as a result of increased competition.

8.9 Assessment Arranging

8.9.1 Yearly Assessment Survey:

Activity Steps: Lead a yearly audit of your expense circumstance. Take advantage of available deductions, optimize your tax strategy, and look into ways to reduce your tax bill.

8.9.2 Change Hold back:

Activity Steps: In the event that you reliably get critical assessment discounts, consider changing your saved portion to build your salary over time.

8.10 Backup stash Recharging

8.10.1 Fast Recharging Plan:

Activity Steps: In the event that you've utilized your secret stash, lay out an arrangement for quick recharging. Continue programmed commitments and allot bonuses towards modifying the asset.

8.10.2 Gain from Withdrawals:

Activity Steps: Evaluate the conditions that prompted the requirement for withdrawal. Utilize this information to refine your just-in-case account objective or change commitments for improved readiness.

8.11 Evaluate Monetary Propensities

8.11.1 Conduct Evaluations:

Activity Steps: Consider your monetary propensities and ways of behaving. Distinguish any examples that might impede your advancement and work towards developing positive monetary propensities.

8.11.2 Look for Responsibility:

Activity Steps: Draw in with a monetary responsibility accomplice or look for help from companions, family, or monetary experts. Open conversations about monetary objectives can give significant points of view and support.

8.12 Stay Educated and Taught

8.12.1 Constant Learning:

Activity Steps: Remain informed about monetary patterns, financial changes, and venture amazing open doors. Nonstop learning upgrades your capacity to pursue informed choices.

8.12.2 Expert Direction:

Activity Steps: Routinely talk with monetary guides. Their skill can give bits of knowledge into market patterns, venture methodologies, and acclimations to your monetary arrangement.

In conclusion, adapting to life changes, maximizing opportunities, and achieving long-term success all depend on constantly monitoring and adjusting your financial plan. By routinely surveying your spending plan, following advancement toward objectives, and remaining informed about economic situations, you position yourself to pursue informed choices and remain on the way to monetary prosperity. Keep in mind, adaptability is critical, and your monetary arrangement ought to advance with your changing conditions and yearnings.

Step 9: Look for Proficient Guidance

Looking for proficient guidance is a reasonable move toward dealing with your funds really. Monetary experts bring ability and experiences that can assist you with exploring complex choices, plan for the future, and upgrade your monetary methodology. When and how to seek professional financial advice are covered in detail in the following guide:

9.1 Recognize When Proficient Exhortation is Required

9.1.1 Complex Monetary Circumstances:

Activity Steps: Look for proficient guidance while confronting complex monetary circumstances, for example, complicated charge arranging, home preparation, or speculation procedures that go past your ability.

9.1.2 Life Advances:

Activity Steps: During significant life changes like marriage, separate, birth of a kid, or retirement, counseling a monetary expert can give important direction to adjusting your monetary arrangement.

9.2 Kinds of Monetary Experts

9.2.1 Affirmed Monetary Organizer (CFP):

Activity Steps: CFPs are prepared to give exhaustive monetary arranging exhortation. Look for their mastery for all encompassing direction on planning, ventures, protection, and retirement arranging.

9.2.2 Financial Consultants:

Activity Steps: Investment portfolio management is the area of expertise of investment advisors. Think about their administrations assuming that you really want help with choosing, observing, and changing your speculations.

9.2.3 Assessment Experts:

Activity Steps: Enroll the assistance of expense experts, like Affirmed Public Bookkeepers (CPAs), for complex duty arranging, planning, and systems to limit charge liabilities.

9.2.4 Domain Arranging Lawyers:

Activity Steps: While managing domain arranging, wills, trusts, and other legitimate issues, talk with bequest arranging lawyers to guarantee your desires are lawfully secured.

9.2.5 Protection Specialists:

Activity Steps: For far reaching protection arranging, including life, wellbeing, and property protection, look for guidance from protection specialists who can fit inclusion to your particular necessities.

9.3 Lead Exploration on Experts

9.3.1 Certifications and Capabilities:

Activity Steps: Research the certifications and capabilities of monetary experts. Search for certificates, licenses, and affiliations that demonstrate an elevated degree of mastery and moral principles.

9.3.2 Client Surveys and Tributes:

Activity Steps: Peruse client audits and tributes to measure the encounters of other people who have worked with the expert. Think about looking for suggestions from confided in companions, family, or partners.

9.4 Starting Interview

9.4.1 Characterize Your Goals:

Activity Steps: Prior to the conference, obviously characterize your monetary goals and regions where you look for help. This helps center the conversation around your particular requirements.

9.4.2 Interrogate:

Activity Steps: Inquire about the professional's approach, experience, and fees during the initial meeting. Examine how they can address your one of a kind monetary circumstance.

9.5 Comprehend Charge Designs

9.5.1 Charge Just Counsels:

Activity Steps: Expense just counselors charge an immediate expense for their administrations and don't procure commissions. Comprehend the expense structure and guarantee it lines up with your inclinations and financial plan.

9.5.2 Commission-Based Consultants:

Activity Steps: Commission-put together counselors gain a commission with appreciation to monetary items they sell. Know about likely irreconcilable circumstances and guarantee straightforwardness in all exchanges.

9.6 Audit and Evaluate Proposals

9.6.1 Point by point Proposals:

Activity Steps: Examine any professional recommendations

carefully following the initial consultation. Guarantee they line up with your monetary objectives and chance resistance.

9.6.2 Evaluate Possible Dangers:

Activity Steps: Analyze the potential dangers posed by the suggested methods. Discuss risk mitigation and, if applicable, inquire about alternative options.

9.7 Second Assessments

9.7.1 Counsel Various Experts:

Activity Steps: Think about looking for second assessments, particularly for critical monetary choices. Various viewpoints can give an all the more balanced perspective on your choices.

9.7.2 Check for Consistency:

Activity Steps: Survey the consistency of suggestions across experts. Consistency can fortify trust in specific procedures or uncover areas of possible concern.

9.8 Lay out a Drawn out Relationship

9.8.1 Continuous Coordinated effort:

Activity Steps: Whenever happy with the underlying conference, consider laying out a drawn out relationship with the expert. Standard registrations consider changes in light of changes in your monetary circumstance.

9.8.2 Correspondence and Availability:

Activity Steps: Guarantee clear correspondence channels and evaluate the openness of the expert. A responsive and informative consultant can address concerns expeditiously.

9.9 Ceaselessly Survey Proficient Connections

9.9.1 Occasional Surveys:

Activity Steps: Intermittently survey your fulfillment with the expert's administrations. Survey whether your monetary necessities are being met and assuming changes in accordance with the relationship are vital.

9.9.2 Advancing Monetary Objectives:

Activity Steps: In the event that your monetary objectives or conditions change, convey these progressions to the expert. A comprehension of your advancing requirements helps tailor guidance likewise.

9.10 Use Innovation and Online Stages

9.10.1 Virtual Meetings:

Activity Steps: Exploit virtual conferences and online stages to associate with monetary experts. This makes it possible to access expertise from a variety of locations with flexibility.

9.10.2 Monetary Arranging Applications:

Activity Steps: Investigate monetary arranging applications that associate you with ensured experts. These stages frequently give planning instruments, speculation following, and simple correspondence with counselors.

9.11 Legitimate and Moral Contemplations

9.11.1 Legitimate Consistence:

Activity Steps: Examine the financial professional's compliance with legal and ethical guidelines. Check their consistence with pertinent administrative bodies and industry affiliations.

9.11.2 Agreements and Disclosures:

Activity Steps: Survey and see any exposures, arrangements, or agreements given by the expert. Look for explanation based on any conditions that might be muddled.

9.12 Instructive Open doors

9.12.1 Monetary Proficiency Studios:

Activity Steps: Go to monetary education studios or courses given by monetary experts. These occasions can upgrade how you might interpret different monetary points and procedures.

9.12.2 Resources for Education:

Activity Steps: Use instructive assets given by monetary experts, including articles, online courses, and pamphlets. Ceaseless learning improves your capacity to settle on informed monetary choices.

All in all, looking for proficient exhortation is a proactive and vital stage in dealing with your funds. Whether managing complex monetary circumstances, significant life changes, or improving your speculation procedure, monetary experts can offer important bits of knowledge and direction. Be persevering in exploring and choosing experts, guarantee straightforwardness in charge structures, and lay out a cooperative relationship that lines up with your monetary objectives. Intermittently survey the viability of the expert relationship and consider changes in view of your developing requirements.

Step 10: Practice Discipline and Persistence

Discipline and persistence are crucial temperance's in making long haul monetary progress. Creating financial wellbeing, overseeing speculations, and arriving at monetary objectives frequently require reliable exertion and an enduring obligation to your monetary arrangement. Here is an extensive aide on the most proficient method to rehearse discipline and persistence in your monetary excursion:

10.1 Develop a Financial Attitude

10.1.1 Recognize Delayed Gratification:

Activity Steps: Embrace the idea of postponed delight. Perceive that forfeiting transient delights can prompt more huge monetary prizes from now on.

10.1.2 Shift Concentration to Long haul Objectives:

Activity Steps: Divert your concentration from quick cravings to long haul monetary objectives. Remember your all-encompassing goals to remain roused and restrained.

10.2 Set Expectations That Are Reasonable

10.2.1 Acknowledge the Long-Term Nature of Success:

Activity Steps: Comprehend that monetary achievement is a drawn out venture. Set practical assumptions and try not to anticipate moment results.

10.2.2 Recognize Market Changes:

Activity Steps: Recognize that there are changes in the financial markets. Try not to settle on incautious choices in light of momentary market developments.

10.3 Adhere to Your Financial plan

10.3.1 Financial plan Adherence:

Activity Steps: Practice discipline by sticking to your spending plan. Oppose the compulsion to overspend and reliably assign assets as per your monetary arrangement.

10.3.2 Regular Audits of the Budget:

Activity Steps: Direct normal audits of your spending plan to guarantee it lines up with your monetary objectives. Change spending classes depending on the situation while keeping a trained methodology.

10.4 Reliable Investment funds Propensities

10.4.1 Mechanized Investment funds:

Activity Steps: To guarantee consistent contributions to your savings objectives, set up automated savings. This trained methodology dispenses with the requirement for manual exchanges.

10.4.2 Treat Reserve funds as Really important:

Activity Steps: Focus on investment funds as a non-debatable cost. Think about it as paying yourself first, supporting the discipline of reliably constructing monetary stores.

10.5 Oppose Close to home Money management

10.5.1 Long haul Venture Point of view:

Activity Steps: When it comes to investing, keep the long term in mind. Fight the temptation to respond sincerely to momentary market variances.

10.5.2 Avoid Timing the Market:

Activity Steps: Teach yourself to stay away from market timing. Reliable, key financial planning frequently outflanks endeavors to foresee transient market developments.

10.6 Tolerance Under water Reimbursement

10.6.1 Follow Obligation Reimbursement Plan:

Activity Steps: Adhere to your obligation reimbursement plan with discipline. Reliably make installments, designate bonuses to obligation decrease, and oppose gathering new obligation.

10.6.2 Recognize Achievements:

Activity Steps: Recognize and celebrate achievements in your obligation reimbursement venture. This encouraging feedback adds to keeping up with discipline and persistence.

10.7.1 Consistent Learning:

Activity Steps: Participate in ceaseless monetary schooling. Remain informed about individual budget, venture procedures, and financial patterns to go with informed choices.

10.7.2 Investigate New Open doors:

Activity Steps: Be available to investigating new monetary open doors. Trained learning permits you to adjust to changing monetary scenes and recognize likely roads for development.

10.8 Keep away from Drive Buys

10.8.1 Lay out a Holding up Period:

Activity Steps: Present a hanging tight period for trivial buys. This training permits you to assess whether a thing is a genuine need or a spur of the moment purchase.

10.8.2 Track and Examine Spur of the moment purchases:

Activity Steps: Keep a record of drive buys. Consistently dissect the rundown to distinguish examples and triggers, supporting restrained ways of managing money.

10.9 Screen and Change Reliably

10.9.1 Ordinary Monetary Registrations:

Activity Steps: Lead standard monetary registrations to screen progress. Your financial plan can be kept in line with your goals if it is regularly evaluated and modified.

10.9.2 Be Available to Variation:

Activity Steps: Develop a mentality of flexibility. Change your monetary techniques in light of changes in your day to day existence, monetary objectives, and outer elements.

10.10 Hug Thriftiness and Effortlessness

10.10.1 Moderation in Spending:

Activity Steps: Embrace a moderate way to deal with spending. Center around what genuinely enhances your life, lessening the requirement for over the top utilization.

10.10.2 Assess Way of life Decisions:

Activity Steps: Intermittently assess your way of life decisions. Survey whether certain costs line up with your qualities and add to your general prosperity.

10.11 Difficulties and Learning's

10.11.1 Acknowledge Difficulties:

Activity Steps: Recognize that failures are a part of every financial journey. Use misfortunes as learning amazing chances to refine your methodology and improve discipline.

10.11.2 Gain from Errors:

Activity Steps: Rather than harping on botches, remove important examples. Make use of what you know about the circumstances that led to the error to avoid repeating them.

10.12 Practice Appreciation

10.12.1 Appreciative Reflection:

Activity Steps: Routinely consider your monetary excursion with appreciation. Celebrate accomplishments, progress, and the beneficial effects of financial discipline.

10.12.2 Happiness Underway:

Activity Steps: Develop satisfaction with the headway you've made. Over time, patience and discipline pay off, and acknowledging your journey helps make things better.